FACES OF
TIME

75 YEARS OF TIME MAGAZINE COVER PORTRAITS

Introduction by **Jay Leno**

A Bulfinch Press Book

in association with the
National Portrait Gallery, Smithsonian Institution

Little, Brown and Company
Boston · New York · Toronto · London

CONTENTS

FOREWORD

Henry Muller

WILL I BE ON THE COVER IN NEW JERSEY?

Jay Leno

PLATES

CHECKLIST

Foreword

THE MOST EAGERLY AWAITED EVENT IN THE EDITORIAL CYCLE AT TIME IS ALWAYS the selection of the cover. Late in the week, usually on Friday night, editors and art directors converge in a conference room to argue the relative importance of major stories, to opine on the artistic and journalistic merits of various images, and finally to hone the cover billings that, one prays, will make the next issue irresistible to readers. Even when the choice of subject matter is easy—who can argue against, say, putting the President-elect on the cover after his victory?—there may be animated debates over which words and image best capture the moment. When there is either no news or too much news, the discussions can go on for hours and the decision can be excruciatingly difficult.

If passions run strong, it is because the cover embodies what TIME is all about: editorial judgment you can trust, clarity and conciseness of expression, aesthetic sensibility—and of course a commercial imperative. Magazines, after all, are sold. So when the debate is over and the managing editor has ruled, the hope is that one has reconciled what sometimes seems irreconcilable. The best covers capture the zeitgeist of the week while surviving the judgment of history. They carry an image that inspires readers to grab the magazine off the newsstand while being worthy of someday being included in a book like this.

Journalism, as the old saying goes, is the first draft of history. What is amazing, as one delves into this volume, is how often the editors got it right. One could do worse than review seventy-five years of TIME covers to recall the events, ideas, and emotions that have defined what the magazine's co-founder, Henry Luce, called the American century. From the beginning, Luce and his fellow editors believed that many stories can best be told through people. Thus cover portraiture became a natural extension of TIME's journalism. As thematic stories became more common, editors and artists rose to the challenge with some of the innovative visual approaches you'll see in this book. The result is that even today, in the age of omnipresent television, networked computers, and screaming tabloid headlines, TIME's words and art collaborate to provide the perspective that brings millions of readers back every week.

One regret I occasionally felt while choosing covers during my years as managing editor of TIME was that two-dimensional representation on a relatively small, red-framed, disposable surface did not always capture the full richness of the works that were delivered to our offices—for example, a globe wrapped by Christo or a delicate lacquered box bearing a portrait of Gorbachev. We are grateful to the National Portrait Gallery for having organized a traveling exhibit that will, in this year of TIME's seventy-fifth birthday, allow many Americans to enjoy the magazine's cover art firsthand just as we editors do. We also thank them for participating in the production of this companion volume, which extends the life of these many remarkable unions of journalism and art beyond the seven days for which they were originally intended.

Henry Muller
Editorial Director, Time Inc.

Will I Be on the Cover in New Jersey?

By Jay Leno

On March 16, 1992, I was on the cover of TIME. When they called to let me know about the decision, I immediately thought of Mort Sahl. I had always been a big fan of Mort, and I knew that he had once been the cover story. That image really made an impression on me because he was the first comedian I could remember being featured on the cover of TIME.

When I called my Mom back in Boston to tell her the news, she said, "Now TIME, which one is that? Is that the one like *People*?"

I explained to her that TIME was the one with "Man of the Year."

She said, "Oh, you mean the red one."

I told her to make sure and call Aunt Fay in New Jersey and all my uncles and cousins in New York, to put them on alert so they could get copies. She said, "You won't be on the magazine down there. They'll only put you on the cover up here because this is your hometown. Somebody else will be on the ones they sell in New Jersey."

I have to admit, before the issue actually arrived, there was a fear factor. It's called "getting bumped." If it happens in comedy clubs and on late-night talk shows, it must happen in the magazine business. TIME has all these plans to put me on the cover, everything is going smoothly, the issue is ready to go to print, a war breaks out somewhere in a country I can't spell or pronounce, and all of a sudden, I'm a sidebar on page 74. Which would have just vindicated my Mom's insistence that each town has a different cover.

When the issue finally came out, my first reaction was selfish. I kept thinking how unfair this was to happen to me at the age of forty-two instead of when I was nineteen. Because being on the cover of TIME just has to be a great way to meet girls. "Would you like to come to my apartment and see the sketch Al Hirschfeld did of me on the cover of TIME?" That's clearly one of the all-time great pickup lines. It certainly beats, "Hi, I'm a sophomore at Emerson, what's your major?"

I remember reading a description, some twenty or twenty-five years ago, of a dinner party TIME had where all the guests were people featured on the cover. How fantastic would it be to attend something like that? If you just take the subjects featured in the National Portrait Gallery's exhibition *Faces of* TIME, the guest list at that dinner party would include eight presidents, five top military leaders, two popes, Churchill, Einstein, and the Beatles.

For better or worse, the cover defines you in popular culture. Because in the information age, in an era when people are bombarded on a daily basis with thousands of facts, figures, and fleeting images, the TIME cover gives 23 million subscribers and countless others a common reference point. For seventy-five years, Americans have talked about, and comedians have poked fun at, the person on the cover. My monologues tend to center on it for one simple reason: a comedian needs no other setup for a joke than to say, "Did you see this week's TIME magazine?" In a diverse culture, the cover is a universally recognized shorthand.

I once heard it said that television is like skywriting. It's there, you see it, and then it's gone. It's true for the viewer—and is also true for the host. I loved doing show number 1299 tonight, and the minute the lights go down, I move on to show number 1300.

Which is one reason being on TIME has been so important to me. That cover, solid in its framed, glossy permanence, is an important milestone in my life. No matter what happens to me in show business, it is something that, ten, twenty, thirty years from now, I can look back upon. Being on the cover is the single most amazing thing to ever happen to me.

Jay Leno by Al Hirschfeld
TIME, March 16, 1992

TIME

Jay
LENO

**Taking over
the throne
after Carson's
remarkable
30-year reign**

*Everything is going smoothly, the issue is ready to go to print, a war breaks out somewhere in
a country I can't spell or pronounce, and all of a sudden, I'm a sidebar on page 74.*

PLATES

Unless otherwise noted,

all artworks are in the collection of, or on loan to,

the National Portrait Gallery, Smithsonian Institution, Washington, D.C.

Names of donors or lenders of specific works are given

in the checklist of the exhibition, page 63.

Text accompanying an artwork appeared originally in the issue of TIME

for which the artwork was the cover illustration.

Charles A. Lindbergh
May. 27, 1927

CHARLES LINDBERGH
Man of the Year

by Samuel J. Woolf
(1880–1948)

charcoal on paper,
33.6 x 28.8 cm
(13¼ x 11¼ in.)

TIME, January 2, 1928

HEROES
Lindbergh

Height: 6 ft. 2 inches.
Age: 25.
Eyes: Blue.
Cheeks: Pink.
Hair: Sandy.

Feet: Large. When he arrived at the Embassy in France no shoes big enough were handy. Habits: Smokes not; drinks not. Does not gamble. Eats a thorough-going breakfast. Prefers light luncheon and dinner when permitted. Avoids rich dishes. Likes sweets.

Calligraphy: From examination of his handwriting Dr. Camille Streletski, Secretary of the French Graphological Society, concluded: superiority, intellectualism, cerebration, idealism, even mysticism.

Characteristics: Modesty, taciturnity, diffidence (women make him blush), singleness of purpose, courage, occasional curtness, phlegm. Elinor Glyn avers he lacks "It."

HENRY PU YI

by Jerry Farnsworth
(1895–1982)

oil on board, 36.2 x 30.5 cm
(14¼ x 12¹⁄₁₆ in.)

TIME, March 5, 1934

In the bitter cold of Manchuria great things were about to happen. . . . Blinking, bespectacled Henry Pu Yi was about to become Manchu emperor of the new state of Ta Manchu Tikuo, until last week Manchukuo. . . . Only 28 years old, Henry Pu Yi is no stranger to thrones. Twice before he has been proclaimed emperor of China. The first time was when he was two years old. . . . In 1917 he became Emperor Hsuan Tung again for a few days when swashbuckling General Hsun . . . captured Peiping, and popped him on the throne in the middle of a July night. . . .

All his life a helpless tool of one agency or another, Pu Yi has longed to dodge the trappings of state and lead the life of a normal western youth. . . . Bicycling is one of his hobbies. As a Japanese puppet he dares not leave his palace unguarded, so he rides around and around his garden compound doing tricks. The emperor of Manchukuo can now pedal on the rear wheel alone, with the front wheel in the air.

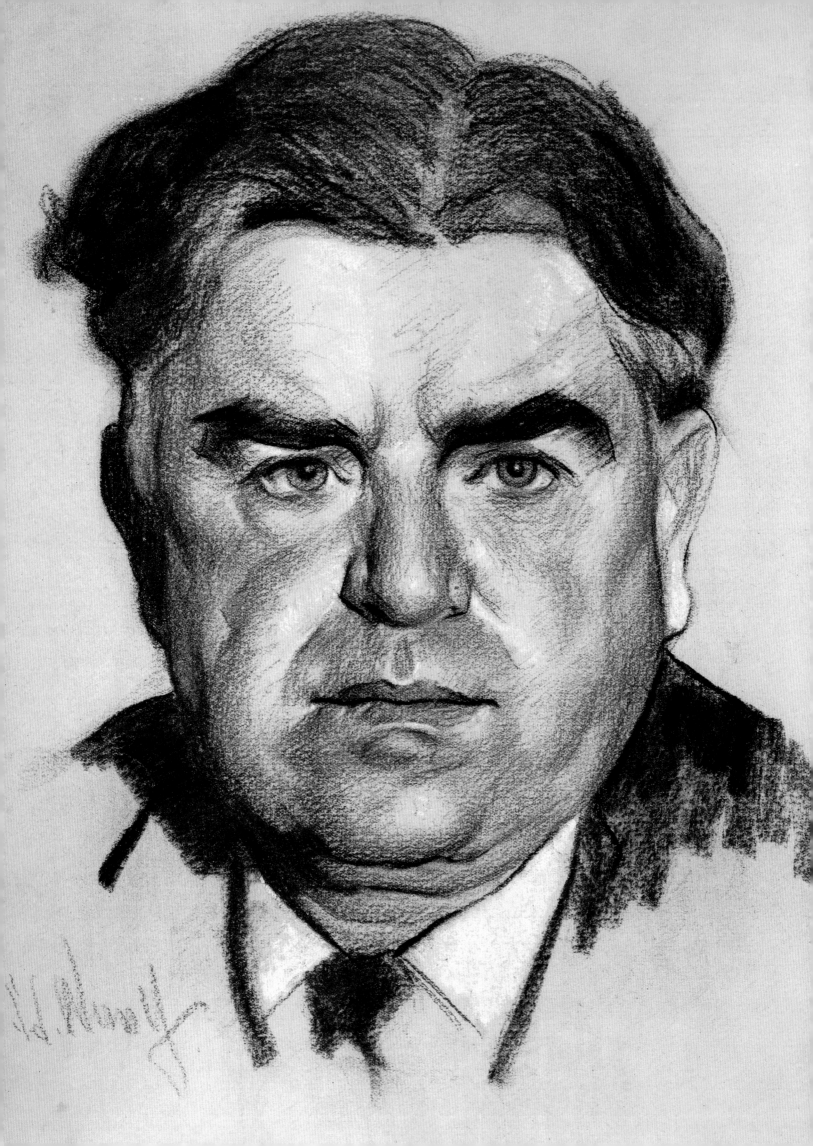

JOHN L. LEWIS

by Samuel J. Woolf
(1880–1948)

charcoal on paper, 32.8 x 27 cm
(12¹⁵⁄₁₆ x 11⅝ in.)

TIME, October 2, 1933

"We will now hear from the president of the United Mine Workers of America."
    . . . Everyone in the hall knew the squat, bull-necked, heavy-pawed figure that swaggered out to the rostrum. There was a glint of arrogance in his grey eyes. He jutted his heavy jaw. Dramatically he introduced himself in the idiom of the true labor leader:
"The name is Lewis—John L."

GERTRUDE STEIN

by George Platt Lynes
(1907–1955)

gelatin silver print, 35.3 x 28.1 cm
(13⅞ x 10¹⁄₁₆ in.)

TIME, September 11, 1933

. . . the plain reader dips into another Stein volume (*Tender Buttons*), to his astonishment brings up these:
"*Red Roses*. A cool red rose and a pink cut pink, a collapse and a sold hole, a little less hot.
"*A Sound*. Elephant beaten with candy and little pops and chews all bolts and reckless rats, this is this. . . .
"*Chicken*. Alas a dirty word, alas a dirty third, alas a dirty bird."
    Some readers laugh, some are annoyed; some snort with disgust or indignation. Gertrude Stein, writer for posterity ("I write for myself and strangers") does not mind. Says she slyly: "My sentences do get under their skin. . . ."

ADMIRAL OSAMI NAGANO

by Boris Artzybasheff
(1899–1965)

gouache on board, 26.6 x 23.3 cm
(10½ x 9³⁄₁₆ in.)

TIME, February 15, 1943

CHIEF OF NAVAL GENERAL STAFF, JAPAN

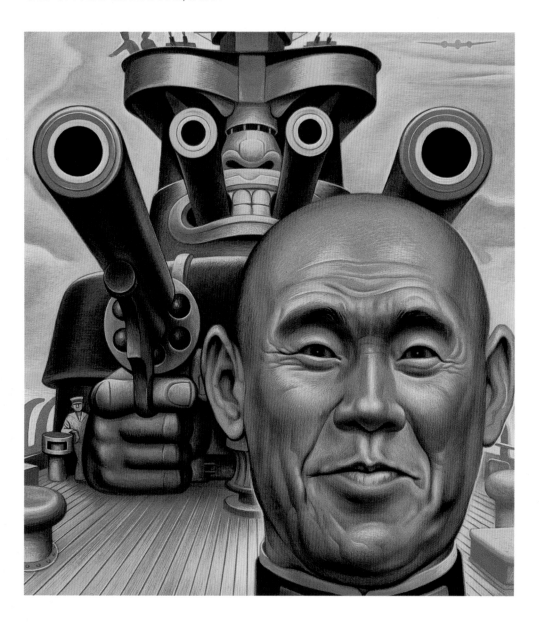

GRAND ADMIRAL KARL DOENITZ

by Boris Artzybasheff
(1899–1965)

gouache on board, 26.8 x 23.9 cm
(10⁹⁄₁₆ x 9⁷⁄₁₆ in.)

TIME, May 10, 1943

COMMANDER IN CHIEF OF THE GERMAN NAVY

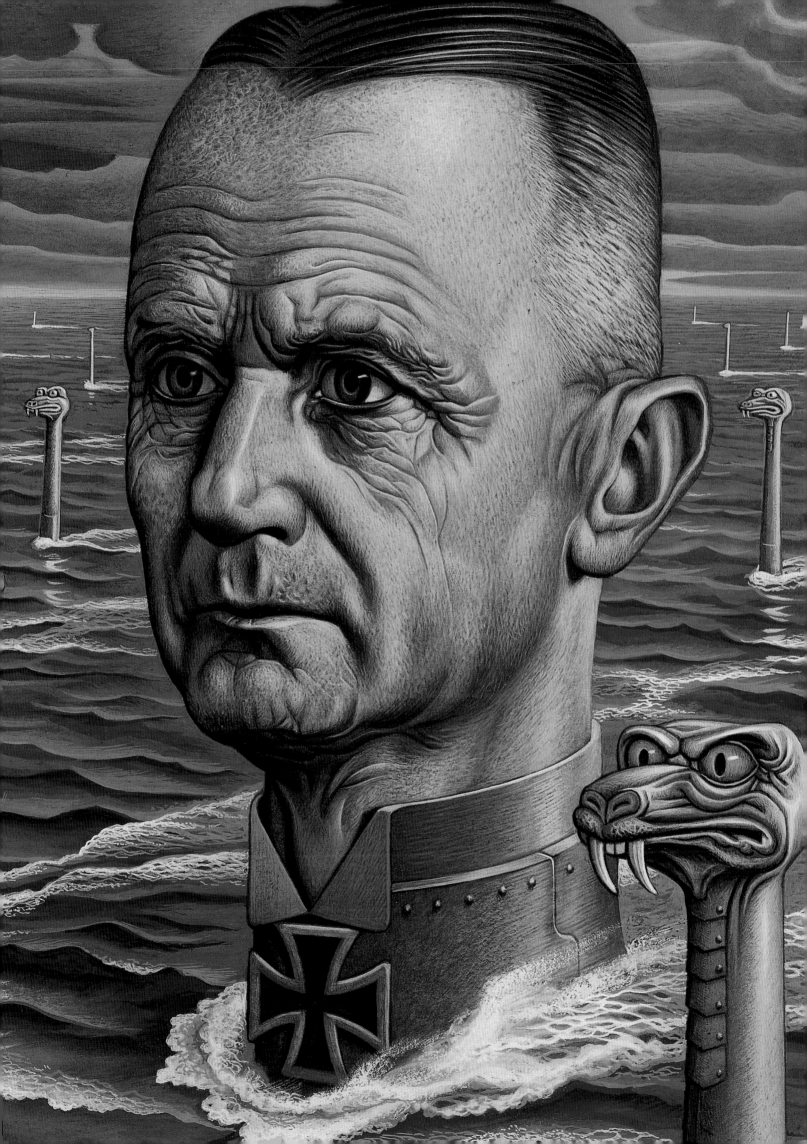

MARSHAL TITO

by Boris Chaliapin
(1904–1979)

gouache on board,
30.4 x 27.2 cm (12 x 10¾ in.)

TIME, October 9, 1944

Word spread through the hills, towns and cities: a remarkable Croat named Tito was fighting the Germans. Yugoslavs from all classes and political parties joined him. . . .

The blacksmith's boy from Klanjec had become leader of a resistance movement that at one time or another pinned down as many as 18 German divisions in fruitless, fraying warfare in the wild Croation and Bosnian mountains.

GENERAL SIR BERNARD LAW MONTGOMERY

by Boris Chaliapin
(1904–1979)

gouache on board, 30.5 x 27.5 cm
(12¹⁄₁₆ x 10⅞ in.)

TIME, February 1, 1943

[Montgomery's] Eighth Army, after some of the bitterest fighting that Egypt had seen, had cracked the Afrika Corps. Newsmen met Montgomery in his desert head-quarters. He sat through the interview with a fly whisk balanced steadily on one finger. "I have defeated the enemy. I am now about to smash him," he asserted flatly, relaxed and asked: "How do you like my hat?" Then wearing a tank corps beret which he had picked up, he climbed into a tank and rumbled off after his troops like a skinny avenging angel.

LIEUTENANT GENERAL JONATHAN WAINWRIGHT

by Ernest Hamlin Baker
(1889–1975)

gouache on board,
25.4 x 22.8 cm (10 x 9 in.)

TIME, May 8, 1944

Shortly before noon, [the] commander of U.S. forces in the Philippines left his headquarters on the stricken island. Wainwright walked toward his conquerors (reported *Nichi Nichi*'s correspondent), carrying a white flag. He "slumped into a chair . . . head held in both hands, his eyes staring at the ground." When the victorious Japanese commander entered the room, "Wainwright and his aides stood up at rigid attention and saluted.". . . It was Corregidor's end. The day was May 6, 1942.

ALBERT EINSTEIN

by Ernest Hamlin Baker
(1889–1975)

gouache on board,
32.8 x 29.2 cm (13 x 11½ in.)

TIME, July 1, 1946

Einstein's discoveries, the greatest
triumph of reasoning mind on
record, are accepted by most
people on faith. Hence the fact
that most people never expect to
understand more about Relativity
than is told by the limerick:

There was a young lady called
  Bright,
Who could travel much faster
  than light;
She went out one day,
In a relative way,
And came back the previous night.

WINSTON CHURCHILL
Man of the Half-Century

by Ernest Hamlin Baker
(1889–1975)

gouache on board,
29.8 x 26.7 cm (11¾ x 10½ in.)

TIME, January 2, 1950

The personal Churchill was happy,
reveling in the good things of life,
both the simple and the complex.
He laid bricks and built dams at
his country home, enjoyed the best
food and sampled, thoroughly,
the best brandy. From painting, for
years his main hobby, he derived
"a tremendous new pleasure."
Only Winston Churchill could have
said: "Painting a picture is like
fighting a battle. . . . It is the same
kind of problem as unfolding a long,
sustained, interlocked argument."

MARIA CALLAS

by Henry Koerner
(1915–1991)

oil on canvas, 55.9 x 71.1 cm
(22 x 28 in.)

TIME, October 29, 1956

Few rate the Callas voice as
opera's sweetest or most
beautiful. It has its ravishing
moments. In quiet passages, it
warms and caresses the air.
In ensembles, it cuts through
the other voices like a
Damascus blade, clean and
strong. . . . But the special
quality of the Callas voice is
not tone. It is the extraordinary
ability to carry, as can no
other, the inflections and
nuances of emotion, from
mordant intensity to hushed
delicacy.

WILLIAM HARTACK

by James Chapin
(1887–1975)

oil on canvas, 51.1 x 35.9 cm
(20⅛ x 14⅛ in.)

TIME, February 10, 1958

If jockeys had their own
colors, his would have to be
red (for guts) and green
(for money).

CHARLES DE GAULLE
Man of the Year

by Bernard Buffet
(born 1928)

oil on canvas,
101 x 74.2 cm
(39¾ x 29¼ in.)

TIME, January 5, 1959

DE GAULLE ON FRANCE:
"The emotional side of me tends to imagine France, like the princess in the fairy stories or the Madonna in the frescoes, as dedicated to an exalted and exceptional destiny. Instinctively I have the feeling that Providence has created her either for complete successes or for exemplary misfortunes. . . . In short, to my mind, France cannot be France without greatness."

DWIGHT D. EISENHOWER

by Andrew Wyeth
(born 1917)

tempera and dry brush on paper,
26.7 x 24.8 cm
(10½ x 9¾ in.)

TIME, September 7, 1959

Los Angeles County
Museum of Art;
gift of Dwight D. Eisenhower
(M.A.)

Ike had always liked Wyeth's work. . . . He found he liked Wyeth's gentle, almost courtly manners too, and permitted him to spend five full days working at Gettysburg. . . . At Wyeth's request Ike donned his favorite jacket, a straw-colored, nubby silk. He sat unsmiling and as if alone with his thoughts. Previous portraitists, working mostly from photographs, have tended to crystallize the popular image of a beamingly paternal president. Wyeth saw and showed an elderly, strong-minded, dedicated public servant, calm in the vortex of great events.

JOHN F. KENNEDY
Man of the Year

by Pietro Annigoni
(1910–1988)

watercolor on paper, 78.5 x 58.7 cm
(30⅞ x 23⅛ in.)

TIME, January 5, 1962

Jack Kennedy . . . had passionately sought the presidency. The closeness of his victory did not disturb him; he took over the office with a youth-can-do-anything sort of self-confidence. He learned better; but learn he did. . . . He also made the process of his growing up to be president a saving factor for the U.S. in the cold war.

POPE JOHN XXIII

by Pietro Annigoni
(1910–1988)

charcoal on paper, 61.6 x 50.1 cm
(24¼ x 19¾ in.)

TIME, October 5, 1962

The purpose of the Second Vatican Council is what His Holiness Pope John XXIII, who has the Catholic prelate's traditional wariness of words that suggest drastic change, calls an *aggiornamento*—a moderniza-tion. This self-reform will affect the life, the worship, and the discipline of every Catholic; just as importantly, it will affect the way the church looks to other Christians, and to the world at large. It is the hope of Pope John, and of many of his bishops, that the Protestant and Orthodox churches will be favorably impressed, and that Catholicism may be pointed toward the far-distant goal of nearly all Christians: their ultimate unity in one church.

VII-VI- LXII
in Vaticano

MARTIN LUTHER KING, JR.
Man of the Year

by Robert Vickrey
(born 1926)

tempera on paper, 37.5 x 28.5 cm
(14¾ x 11¼ in.)

TIME, January 3, 1964

MARTIN LUTHER KING, JR.

by Ben Shahn
(1898–1969)

pen, ink, and wash on
Japanese paper,
66.6 x 51.7 cm
(26¼ x 20⅜ in.)

TIME, March 19, 1965

Amon Carter Museum,
Fort Worth, Texas

Ben Shahn is as famed in his own medium of protest as King is in his. Lately he has been contributing posters and lithographs to various civil rights groups. . . . He saw his subject mainly as an orator. "This is King today," he said. "He isn't as placid as he was a year ago. I admire the man immensely. He has moved more people by his oratory than anyone else I can think of."

BUCKMINSTER FULLER

by Boris Artzybasheff
(1899–1965)

tempera on board,
54.6 x 43.2 cm (21½ x 17 in.)

TIME, January 10, 1964

He has been called "the first poet of technology," "the greatest living genius of industrial-technical realization in building," "an anticipator of the world to come—which is different from being a prophet," "a seminal thinker," and "an inspired child." But all these encomiums are fairly recent. For most of his life, R. Buckminster Fuller was known simply as a crackpot.

He is also something more. . . . He is a throwback to the classic American individualist, a mold which produced Thomas Edison and Thoreau—men with the fresh eye that sees and questions everything anew, and the crotchety mind that refuses to believe there is anything that cannot be done.

THELONIOUS MONK

by Boris Chaliapin
(1904–1979)

oil on canvas, 53.6 x 38.1 cm
(21⅛ x 15 in.)

TIME, February 28, 1964

Monk's lifework of 57 compositions is a diabolical and witty self-portrait, a string of stark snapshots of his life in New York. Changing meters, unique harmonies, and oddly voiced chords create the effect of a desperate conversation in some other language, a fit of drunken laughter, a shout from a park at night. His melodies make mocking twins of naiveté and cynicism, of ridicule and fond memory. . . . Monk himself plays with deliberate incaution, attacking the piano as if it were a carillon's keyboard or a finely tuned set of 88 drums. The array of sounds he divines from his Baldwin grand are beyond the reach of academic pianists; he caresses a note with the tremble of a bejeweled finger, then stomps it into its grave with a crash of elbow and forearm aimed with astonishing accuracy at a chromatic tone cluster an octave long.

JEANNE MOREAU

by Rufino Tamayo
(1899–1991)

charcoal, pencil, and
crayon on paper
72.4 x 57.2 cm
(28½ x 22½ in.)

TIME, March 5, 1965

Instead of the flamboyant, movie-star type [Rufino Tamayo] had envisaged, the artist found his subject "a most unglamorous girl of marvelous simplicity. From the beginning," he recalled of the sittings in his Cuernavaca weekend home, "she said we should talk in English because her mother was English and she preferred the maternal tongue. It was her own delightful way of telling me what I already knew—that my French is preposterous." . . . The Tamayo portrait . . . stirred mixed feelings in the subject. Said Jeanne: "I was struck by one thing when I saw the portrait [in progress], and that was the strength he found in me—not the strength I have, but the strength I would like to have."

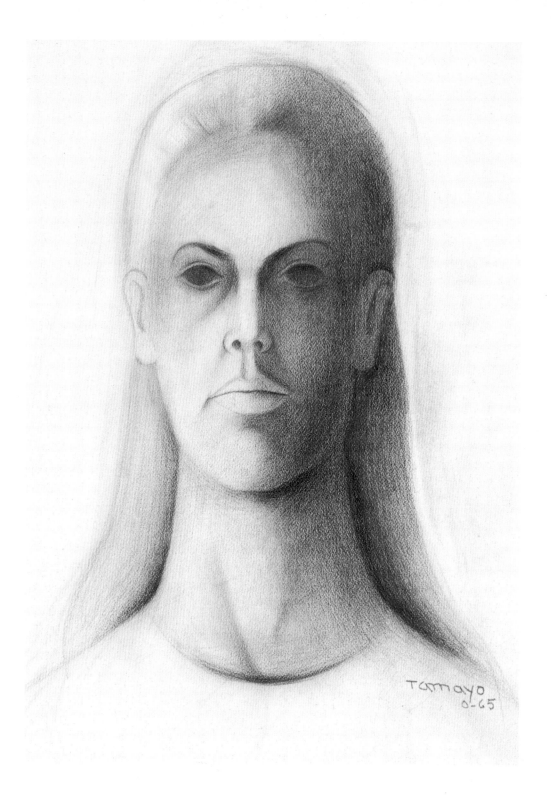

RUDOLF NUREYEV

by Sidney Nolan
(1917–1992)

acrylic on board, 124.4 x 124.4 cm
(49 x 49 in.)

TIME, April 16, 1965

An Australian who now lives in London, [Sidney] Nolan is known for his brooding canvases, his translucent color, and his figures of man, often puzzled but always dignified. . . . He is a convinced Nureyev fan, has been observing the dancer since 1962. In London he once watched from the balcony for a week while Nureyev was rehearsing for *Romeo and Juliet,* a ballet that Nolan sees as "a ritual description of our civilization." The portrait depicts Nureyev in rehearsal costume, a kerchief round his head. "I wanted to show the feeling I got from him as he rehearsed Romeo," Nolan said. "He is a wonderfully perceptive artist, and I tried to get that in as well."

THE BEATLES

*by Gerald Scarfe
(born 1936)*

*papier-mâché and cloth grouping,
approx. 120 x 130 x 100 cm
(47¼ x 51¼ x 39⅜ in.)*

TIME, September 22, 1967

In case you weren't exactly sure, the way they are arranged on the cover, left to right, is George, Ringo, Paul, and John. This view of the Beatles is the work of Gerald Scarfe, 31, the British cartoonist/satirist whose grotesque caricatures in the British press . . . have been the nemesis of the high, mighty, and famous, from Lyndon Johnson to Queen Elizabeth. . . .

Scarfe started by sketching Ringo at the drummer's London suburban home, raced back to his Thames-side studio to construct a likeness on a wire frame with papier-mâché made of old newspapers soaked in paste. He followed the same process for all four. The figures are life-size head-and-torso, with paper-and-glue eyeballs inserted from the rear of the framework, hair made of scissors-fringed strips of the London *Daily Mail*, and a final facial of thin paste and watercolor. Each unclad figure took two days to build. . . .

Scarfe, who admires the creativity and force of the Beatles' music and is similarly admired by them, says that he "was trying to catch them as they are at present. They have moved on since *Sgt. Pepper*—the drug thing—to the meditation scene." Notable

among the flowers, all of which are real, is the rose held by Paul, who told Scarfe that the Beatles' own guru, Maharishi Mahesh Yogi, once gave him a rose with this parable: "Here are the petals of the rose. Here is the stalk of the rose. But none of these is the real rose. The real rose is the sap." "And that," said Paul to Scarfe, "is what we are all looking for."

ROBERT LOWELL

by Sidney Nolan
(1917–1992)

watercolor and gouache on paper, 30.5 x 25.4 cm (12 x 10 in.)

TIME, June 2, 1967

"There's poetry all over the place," says Robert Lowell. "The world is swimming with it. I think more people write it, and there are more ways to write it. It's almost pointless—there's no money in it—but a lot of them become teachers, and a lot of them write quite good poems and read to a lot of people. Poets are a more accepted part of society, and I don't know if it's bad for us or not, but it's pleasanter. . . . Still, being good isn't any easier."

Robert Lowell, 50, is better than good. As far as such a judgment can ever be made of a working, living artist, he is, by rare critical consensus, the best American poet of his generation.

The bulk of his best poetry is seared with a fiery desperation, fed by rage and self-laceration. The world's ills become his own, and his own the world's:

I hear
My ill-spirit
Sob in each blood cell,
As if my hand were at its
    throat . . .
I myself am hell.

LYNDON JOHNSON
Man of the Year

by Peter Hurd
(1904–1984)

tempera on paper,
55.2 x 37.5 cm
(21¾ x 14¾ in.)

TIME, January 1, 1965

PRESIDENT OF THE
UNITED STATES

L.B.J. AS LEAR
Man of the Year

by David Levine
(born 1926)

ink on board, 26.7 x 18.8 cm
(10½ x 7⅜ in.)

TIME, January 5, 1968

opposite:
LYNDON B. JOHNSON

by Pietro Annigoni
(1910–1988)

pastel on paper,
48.5 x 38.1 cm
(19⅛ x 15 in.)

TIME, April 12, 1968

34

P. Annigoni Att
XV - X - LXVI

ROBERT KENNEDY

by Roy Lichtenstein
(1923–1997)

lithograph,
50.8 x 36.7 cm
(20 x 14⁷/₁₆ in.)

TIME, May 24, 1968

Pop artist Roy Lichtenstein . . . says that Kennedy is one of the very few real people he has ever portrayed. The 44-year-old artist usually turns out comic-strip-style superheroes with square jaws and their girlfriends with superperfect coiffures. What he liked most about Kennedy, he says, was his "lively, upstart quality and pop-heroic proportions as part of a legend."

THE GUN IN AMERICA

by Roy Lichtenstein
(1923–1997)

lithograph,
51 x 36.7 cm
(20¹/₈ x 14⁷/₁₆ in.)

TIME, June 21, 1968

TIME magazine,
New York City

RAQUEL WELCH

by Frank Gallo
(born 1933)

epoxy resin, 106 x 46.6 x 24.1 cm
(41¾ x 18⁵/₁₆ x 9½ in.)

TIME, November 28, 1969

The sculpture took three weeks to complete, and Gallo personally brought it from Champaign, Illinois, to New York—it sat beside him wrapped in a first-class Ozark Air Lines seat. At first the package was too bulky to get the seat belt around, so Gallo was obliged to unwrap it. That caused quite a stir on the plane.

BOB HOPE

by Marisol
(born 1930)

polychromed wood,
48.2 x 38 x 40.6 cm
(19 x 15 x 16 in.)

TIME, December 22, 1967

They'd know that jaunty saunter anywhere. Bob Hope comes onstage with the cocky glide of a golfer who has just knocked off three birdies for a 68 and nailed Arnold Palmer to the clubhouse door. The crooked grin spreads wide, the clear brown eyes stay cool, and the audience roars its welcome; they can hardly wait for Hope to sock it to them. And so he does. Five, six gags a minute. Pertinent, impertinent, leering, perishing. . . . When he misses, the famous scooped snoot shoots defiantly skyward, the prognathous jaw drops in mock anguish, or he goes into a stop-action freeze. Sometimes he just repeats the line until the audience gets it. They have to laugh of course—but if they don't, it's almost treason.

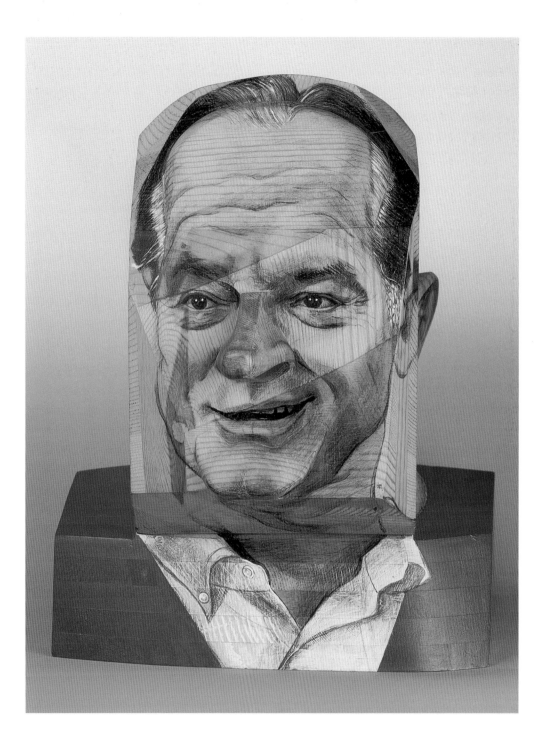

JESSE JACKSON

*by Jacob Lawrence
(born 1917)*

*tempera on board,
60.3 x 45.7 cm
(23¾ x 18 in.)*

TIME, April 6, 1970

CIVIL RIGHTS LEADER

KATE MILLET

*by Alice Neel
(1900–1984)*

*acrylic on canvas,
102.2 x 74.2 cm
(40⅜ x 29³⁄₁₆ in.)*

TIME, August 31, 1970

Until this year, . . . the [feminist] movement had no coherent theory to buttress its intuitive passions, no ideologue to provide chapter and verse for its assaults on patriarchy. Kate Millet, 35, a sometime sculptor and longtime brilliant misfit in a man's world, has filled the role through *Sexual Politics.*

In a way, the book has made Millet the Mao Tse-tung of Women's Liberation. That is the sort of description she and her sisters despise, for the movement rejects the notion of leaders and heroines as creations of the media—and mimicry of the ways that men use to organize their world.

TED KENNEDY

*by Larry Rivers
(born 1923)*

*pencil and wood collage,
29.2 x 21.6 cm
(11½ x 8½ in.)*

TIME, November 29, 1971

UNITED STATES SENATOR
EDWARD KENNEDY

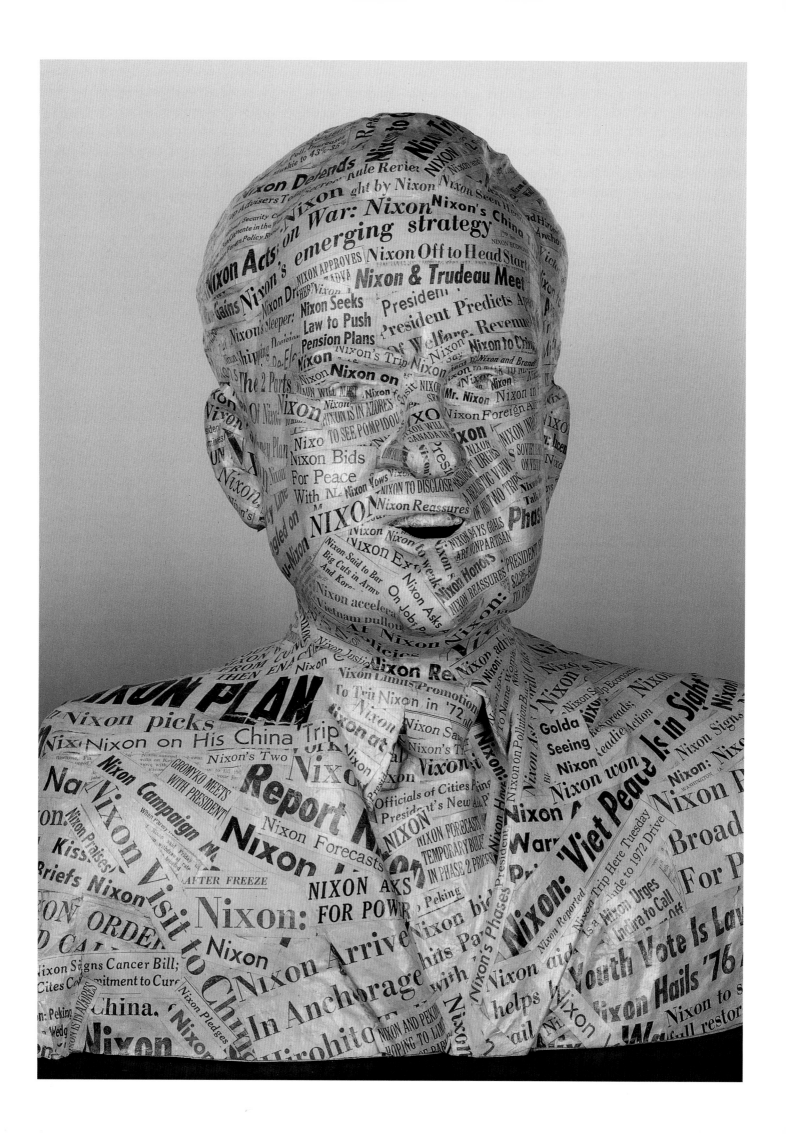

RICHARD NIXON
Man of the Year

by Stanley Glaubach
(1925–1973)

papier-mâché sculpture,
50.8 x 53.6 x 27.3 cm
(20 x 21⅛ x 10¾ in.)

TIME, January 3, 1972

WATERGATE BREAKS WIDE OPEN

by Jack Davis
(born 1926)

watercolor and ink on board,
53.3 x 48.5 cm (21 x 19⅛ in.)

TIME, April 30, 1973

AYATULLAH
RUHOLLAH KHOMEINI
Man of the Year

by Brad Holland
(born 1944)

oil on canvas,
27.9 x 20.3 cm
(11 x 8 in.)

TIME, January 7, 1980

LEADER OF THE
IRANIAN REVOLUTION

JIMMY CARTER

Man of the Year

by James Wyeth
(born 1946)

watercolor on paper,
35.5 x 28 cm
(14 x 11 1/16 in.)

TIME, January 3, 1977

Just a year ago, he was walking up to men and women who did not know he existed, shaking their hands, and drawling, "I'm Jimmy Carter, and I'm going to be your next president." The political professionals were dead sure he did not have a chance—but none of the voters laughed in his face. He was such an engaging man—a trifle shy, for all his gall, and there was that sunburst of a smile that people would always remember. Right from the start, he was perceived as being a rather different kind of politician compared with the rest of the field—as different in philosophy and tactics . . . as in personal style. He not only knew what he wanted; he also sensed, at least in the primary elections, what the American people wanted.

The result was something of a political miracle.

JOHN GOTTI

by Andy Warhol
(1928–1987)

silkscreen on colored paper,
82.5 x 63.5 cm (32½ x 25 in.)

TIME, September 29, 1986

HEAD OF THE GAMBINO CRIME
FAMILY, NEW YORK

MICHAEL JACKSON

by Andy Warhol
(1928–1987)

oil and silkscreen on canvas,
76.1 x 66.1 cm
(29¹⁵⁄₁₆ x 26 ¹⁄₁₆ in.)

TIME, March 19, 1984

Many observers find in the
ascendancy of Michael Jackson
the ultimate personification of
the androgynous rock star. His
high-flying tenor makes him
sound like the lead in some
funked-up boys choir, even as the
sexual dynamism irradiating from
the arch of his dancing body
challenges government standards
for a nuclear meltdown. His lithe
frame, five-fathom eyes, long
lashes might be threatening if
Jackson gave, even for a second,
the impression that he is obtainable.
But the audience's sense of his
sensuality becomes quite deliberately
tangled with the mirror image
of his life: the good boy, the
God-fearing Jehovah's Witness,
the adamant vegetarian, the
resolute non-indulger in smoke,
strong drink, or dope of any kind,
the impossibly insulated innocent.
Undeniably sexy. Absolutely safe.
Eroticism at arm's length.

RONALD REAGAN
Man of the Year

by Aaron Shikler
(born 1922)

essence of oil on paper,
66 x 45.5 cm (26 x 17⅞ in.)

TIME, January 5, 1981

If one were to take all of Reagan's qualities—the detachment, the self-knowledge, the great voice and good looks—and project them into the White House, he would have a first-class B-movie presidency. That is no insult. The best B movies, while not artistically exquisite, are often the ones that move us most because they move us directly, through straightforward characters, simple moral conflicts and idealized talk.

PAUL "BEAR" BRYANT

by Neil Leifer
(born 1943)

color photograph,
35.6 x 28 cm (14 x 11 in.)

TIME, September 29, 1980

To the rabid, almost reverential followers of his University of Alabama football teams, Paul William "Bear" Bryant is a nearly mythic figure, a man who embodies the traditional American values: dedication, hard work, honesty, and, above all, success. To the frustrated fans of the legions of teams he has defeated, he is a relentlessly slippery recruiter, a ruthless win-at-all-costs tyrant. To some, he is the demigod of the autumn religion, the finest coach of a uniquely American game. To others, he is the proselytizer of a brutal sport, a symbol of a national fixation on violence.

LECH WALESA
Man of the Year

by Jim Dine
(born 1935)

charcoal and pencil on paper
and photo montage,
25.7 x 36.1 cm (10⅛ x 14¼ in.)

TIME, January 4, 1982

Anyone could read him at a glance. When things were going well, when it seemed for a while that the movement he led would brighten and liberate the lives of his fellow Poles, the face that grew so familiar in 1981 radiated delight: delight in his crusade, delight in his vision of the future, delight in being at the center of it all. In those moments, he held nothing back. But when things began to go wrong, when the tensions started to rise and the future he saw began to recede, the face grew heavy. The familiar walrus mustache sagged and the brown eyes turned weary. Again he held nothing back, and perhaps he could not if he tried. Lech Walesa is a man of emotion, not of logic or analysis. So was this movement, which he all but lost control of in the end, guided more by hope and passion than by rationality. That was the crusade's strength—and its weakness.

JOHN UPDIKE

by Alex Katz
(born 1927)

*oil on canvas, 122.5 x 86.7 cm
(48¼ x 34⅛ in.)*

TIME, October 18, 1982

"Among artists, a writer's equipment is least out-of-reach—the language we all more or less use, a little patience at grammar and spelling, the common adventures of blundering mortals. A painter must learn to paint; his studio is redolent of alchemic substances and physical force. The musician's arcanum of specialized knowledge and personal dexterity is even more intimidating, less accessible to the untrained, and therefore somehow less corruptible than the writer's craft. Though some painters and musicians go bad in the prime of their lives, far fewer do, and few so drastically, as writers. Our trick is treacherously thin; our art is so incorrigibly amateur that novices constantly set the world of letters on its ear, and the very phrase 'professional writer' has a grimy sound. Hilaire Belloc said that the trouble with writing was that it was never meant to be a profession, it was meant to be a hobby. An act of willful play."
—*John Updike*

RONALD REAGAN AND YURI ANDROPOV
Men of the Year

by Alfred Leslie
(born 1927)

oil on canvas, 152.4 x 137.2 cm
(60 x 54 in.)

TIME, January 2, 1984

[T]here is a grave danger: if not of war tomorrow, then of a long period of angry immobility in superpower relations; of an escalating arms race bringing into U.S. and Soviet arsenals weapons ever more expensive and difficult to control; of rising tension that might make every world trouble spot a potential flash point for the clash both sides fear. The deterioration of U.S.–Soviet relations to that frozen impasse overshadowed all other events of 1983. In shaping plans for the future, every states- man in the world and very nearly every private citizen has to calculate what may come of the face-off between the countries whose leaders — one operating in full public view, the other as a mysterious presence hidden by illness — share the power to decide whether there will be any future at all. Those leaders, Presidents Ronald Wilson Reagan of the United States and Yuri Vladimirovich Andropov of the Union of Soviet Socialist Republics, are TIME's Men of the Year.

JESSE HELMS

by Alfred Leslie
(born 1927)

oil on canvas, 46.3 x 34.2 cm
(18¼ x 13½ in.)

TIME, September 14, 1981

UNITED STATES SENATOR
One recent afternoon he was at home [in Raleigh, North Carolina], slouched in a living-room chair, feet in $7 mail-order sneakers flat on the floor. His dog Patches, essentially a beagle, quivered under the couch. Helms emptied his pockets — some change, a silver cross, a Christian medallion — and talked about his curious perch in American politics. "Some folks say I'm scary," he says. "The people here don't think I'm scary."

VLADIMIR HOROWITZ

by R. B. Kitaj
(born 1932)

pastel on paper, 57.1 x 39 cm
(22½ x 15⅜ in.)

TIME, May 5, 1986

When he arrived in Moscow last
week, a Soviet official asked to
see some identification. "My face
is my passport," replied Vladimir
Horowitz, 81, returning to his
homeland for the first time since
he fled to the West 61 years ago.
The pianist, who is to perform
two concerts in Moscow and
Leningrad under a new U.S.–Soviet
cultural exchange . . . clearly retains
a special place in the hearts of the
Soviet people. A two-hour rehearsal
in the Great Hall of Moscow's
conservatory left 1,600 spectators
cheering wildly.

DAVID BYRNE

by David Byrne
(born 1952)

photo collage, 40.6 x 30.3 cm
(16 x 11¹⁵/₁₆ in.)

TIME, October 27, 1986

LEAD SINGER AND SONGWRITER OF
THE ROCK BAND TALKING HEADS,
COMPOSER, AND DIRECTOR OF THE
FILM *TRUE STORIES* (1986)

MIKHAIL GORBACHEV
Man of the Year

by Nikolai Soloninkin
(born 1945)

papier-mâché box,
15.3 x 12.1 x 5.2 cm
(6 x 4¾ x 2¹/₁₆ in.)

TIME, January 4, 1988

TIME magazine, New York City

Most readers may not recognize the style of painting employed for this week's Man of the Year cover portrait, but Mikhail Gorbachev and his fellow Soviets certainly will. The image is actually the top of a lacquered box. For more than 200 years, artisans in a handful of villages in northern Russia have been turning out such delicately painted artifacts. The boxes have attracted collectors around the world. . . .

Linda Jackson, wife of Moscow bureau chief James O. Jackson and a collector of the boxes, . . . journeyed 24 miles north of Moscow to the village of Fedoskino. There she found Nikolai Soloninkin, who holds the title of "merited artist" at the town's famous miniature-painting studio. Artisans of Fedoskino and the nearby village of Danilkovo are believed to have originated the genre, and their exquisitely rendered village scenes and portraiture remain unparalleled. Soloninkin, 42, spent ten days painting Gorbachev's likeness on a 4¾-in. by 6-in. papier-mâché box that had been slow baked in a 212 degrees F oven for nearly a month, and then covered with four coats of lacquer. The artist, who worked from stacks of news photographs, developed a rapport with his subject. "I really like the man," he says. "To me, he is much more an ordinary, down-to-earth person than some other leaders."

DENG XIAOPING
Man of the Year

by Robert Rauschenberg
(born 1925)

photo collage,
49.5 x 35.5 cm
(19½ x 14 in.)

TIME, January 6, 1986

LEADER OF CHINA
Deng's long career has been a biographer's dream, a tumultuous charge through war and revolution, exhilarating political triumphs and equally humiliating downfalls, personal achievements and family tragedies. Through it all, drawing on seemingly limitless reserves of energy and wily resilience, the tenacious 4-ft. 11-in. politician has managed not only to endure but to prevail. Today, one year into his ninth decade, he stands at the zenith of his power as leader of the world's most populous nation and as progenitor of what he proudly calls its "second revolution."

I LOVE NEW YORK

by Roger Brown
(1941–1997)

oil on canvas, 127 x 96.5 cm
(50 x 38 in.)

TIME, September 17, 1990

TIME magazine, New York City

WRAPPED GLOBE, 1988
Planet of the Year
by Christo
(born 1935)
photograph by
Gianfranco Gorgoni

plastic, polyethylene rope,
and globe,
45.1 cm (17¾ in.) diameter

TIME, January 2, 1989

TIME magazine,
New York City

This week's unorthodox choice of Endangered Earth as Planet of the Year, in lieu of the usual Man or Woman of the Year, had its origin in the scorching summer of 1988, when environmental disasters—droughts, floods, forest fires, polluted beaches—dominated the news.

While a team of writers and researchers worked on the stories back in New York City, art director Rudy Hoglund and deputy director Arthur Hochstein, who designed the layouts for the entire package, faced a difficult problem: how to create a strikingly original cover image. Their solution was to approach Christo, the famed Bulgarian-born environmental sculptor. In earlier works Christo had draped in plastic large sections of the earth—a stretch of Australian coast, a canyon in Colorado—but never the whole planet. This time Christo bundled a 16-in. globe in polyethylene and rag rope and drove more than 350 miles up and down New York's Long Island in search of the perfect combination of light, air, and sea for a photograph. The result—*Wrapped Globe 1988*—is a fitting symbol of earth's vulnerability to man's reckless ways.

WOMEN: THE ROAD AHEAD

by Susan Moore (born 1953)

oil pastel, paint stick, acrylic on paper,
208.3 x 182.9 cm (82 x 72 in.)

TIME, special issue, fall 1990

TIME magazine, New York City

BILL CLINTON

by C. F. Payne
(born 1954)

watercolor, ink, acrylic, and
oil on board,
41.9 x 33 cm (16 ½ x 13 in.)

TIME, February 22, 1993

POPE JOHN PAUL II
Man of the Year

by Richard Selesnick and
Nicholas Kahn
(both born 1964)

fresco, 45.7 x 35.5 cm
(18¾ x 14 in.)

TIME, January 2, 1995

TIME magazine, New York City

. . . John Paul expressed thanks
[for being chosen Man of the

Year] then added mischievously,
"I see that in the past, you have
given this honor to Lech Walesa
and to Pope John XXIII—but also
to Stalin and Hitler!" [TIME bureau
chief Thomas] Sancton, a bit
nonplussed, explained,
"Holy Father, you must understand
that we have a good list and
a bad list. You are on the good
list." Gratified but still playful, the
Pontiff replied, "I hope I always
remain on the good list."

CHECKLIST

Unless otherwise noted, all items are owned by the National Portrait Gallery, Smithsonian Institution, Washington, D.C.; gift of TIME magazine.

Charles Lindbergh 1902–1974
Man of the Year
by Samuel J. Woolf (1880–1948)
charcoal on paper
TIME, January 2, 1928
National Portrait Gallery, Smithsonian Institution, Washington, D.C.; on loan from Germantown Friends School, Philadelphia, Pennsylvania

John L. Lewis 1880–1969
by Samuel J. Woolf (1880–1948)
charcoal on paper
TIME, October 2, 1933

Gertrude Stein 1874–1946
by George Platt Lynes (1907–1955)
gelatin silver print
TIME, September 11, 1933

Henry P'u Yi 1906–1967
by Jerry Farnsworth (1895–1982)
oil on board
TIME, March 5, 1934

**General Sir
Bernard Law Montgomery**
1906–1967
by Boris Chaliapin (1904–1979)
gouache on board
TIME, February 1, 1943
National Portrait Gallery, Smithsonian Institution, Washington, D.C.; gift of Mrs. Boris Chaliapin

**Lieutenant General
Jonathan Wainwright** 1883–1953
by Ernest Hamlin Baker (1889–1975)
gouache on board
TIME, May 8, 1944
National Portrait Gallery, Smithsonian Institution, Washington, D.C.; purchased with funds from Rosemary Frankeberger

Admiral Osami Nagano 1880–1947
by Boris Artzybasheff (1899–1965)
gouache on board
TIME, February 15, 1943

Grand Admiral Karl Doenitz
1891–1981
by Boris Artzybasheff (1899–1965)
gouache on board
TIME, May 10, 1943

Marshal Tito 1892–1980
by Boris Chaliapin (1904–1979)
gouache on board
TIME, October 9, 1944
National Portrait Gallery, Smithsonian Institution, Washington, D.C.; gift of Mrs. Boris Chaliapin

Albert Einstein 1879–1955
by Ernest Hamlin Baker (1889–1975)
gouache on board
TIME, July 1, 1946

Winston Churchill 1874–1965
Man of the Half-Century
by Ernest Hamlin Baker (1889–1975)
gouache on board
TIME, January 2, 1950

Maria Callas 1923–1977
by Henry Koerner (1915–1991)
oil on canvas
TIME, October 29, 1956

William Hartack born 1932
by James Chapin (1887–1975)
oil on canvas
TIME, February 10, 1958

Charles De Gaulle 1890–1970
Man of the Year
by Bernard Buffet (born 1928)
oil on canvas
TIME, January 5, 1959

Dwight D. Eisenhower 1890–1969
by Andrew Wyeth (born 1917)
tempera and dry brush on paper
TIME, September 7, 1959
Los Angeles County Museum of Art, California; gift of Dwight D. Eisenhower (M.A.)

John F. Kennedy 1917–1963
Man of the Year
by Pietro Annigoni (1910–1988)
watercolor on paper
TIME, January 5, 1962

Pope John XXIII 1881–1963
by Pietro Annigoni (1910–1988)
charcoal on paper
TIME, October 5, 1962

Martin Luther King, Jr. 1929–1968
Man of the Year
by Robert Vickrey (born 1926)
tempera on paper
TIME, January 3, 1964

Buckminster Fuller 1895–1983
by Boris Artzybasheff (1899–1965)
tempera on board
TIME, January 10, 1964

Thelonious Monk 1917–1982
by Boris Chaliapin (1904–1979)
oil on canvas
TIME, February 28, 1964

Martin Luther King, Jr. 1929–1968
by Ben Shahn (1898–1969)
pen, ink, and wash on Japanese paper
TIME, March 19, 1965
Amon Carter Museum, Fort Worth, Texas

Jeanne Moreau born 1928
by Rufino Tamayo (1899–1991)
charcoal, pencil, and crayon on paper
TIME, March 5, 1965

Lyndon Johnson 1908–1973
Man of the Year
by Peter Hurd (1904–1984)
tempera on paper
TIME, January 1, 1965

Rudolf Nureyev 1938–1993
by Sidney Nolan (1917–1992)
acrylic on board
TIME, April 16, 1965

Robert Lowell 1917–1977
by Sidney Nolan (1917–1992)
watercolor and gouache on paper
TIME, June 2, 1967

The Beatles
George Harrison, born 1943;
Ringo Starr, born 1940;
Paul McCartney, born 1942;
John Lennon, 1940–1980
by Gerald Scarfe (born 1936)
papier-mâché and cloth grouping
TIME, September 22, 1967

Bob Hope born 1903
by Marisol (born 1930)
polychromed wood
TIME, December 22, 1967

"L. B. J. as Lear" 1908–1973
Man of the Year
by David Levine (born 1926)
ink on board
TIME, January 5, 1968

Lyndon B. Johnson 1908–1973
by Pietro Annigoni (1910–1988)
pastel on paper
TIME, April 12, 1968

Robert Kennedy 1925–1968
by Roy Lichtenstein (1923–1997)
lithograph
TIME, May 24, 1968

"The Gun in America"
by Roy Lichtenstein (1923–1997)
lithograph
TIME, June 21, 1968
TIME *magazine, New York City*

Raquel Welch born 1940
by Frank Gallo (born 1933)
epoxy resin
TIME, November 28, 1969

Jesse Jackson born 1941
by Jacob Lawrence (born 1917)
tempera on board
TIME, April 6, 1970

Kate Millet born 1934
by Alice Neel (1900–1984)
acrylic on canvas
TIME, August 31, 1970

Ted Kennedy born 1932
by Larry Rivers (born 1923)
pencil and wood collage
TIME, November 29, 1971

Richard Nixon 1913–1994
Man of the Year
by Stanley Glaubach (1925–1973)
papier-mâché sculpture
TIME, January 3, 1972

"Watergate Breaks Wide Open"
by Jack Davis (born 1926)
watercolor and ink on board
TIME, April 30, 1973

Jimmy Carter born 1924
Man of the Year
by James Wyeth (born 1946)
watercolor on paper
TIME, January 3, 1977

Ayatullah Ruhollah Khomeini
1900–1989
Man of the Year
by Brad Holland (born 1944)
oil on canvas
TIME, January 7, 1980

Paul "Bear" Bryant 1913–1973
by Neil Leifer (born 1943)
color photograph
TIME, September 29, 1980

Ronald Reagan born 1911
Man of the Year
by Aaron Shikler (born 1922)
essence of oil on paper
TIME, January 5, 1981

Jesse Helms born 1921
by Alfred Leslie (born 1927)
oil on canvas
TIME, September 14, 1981

Lech Walesa born 1943
Man of the Year
by Jim Dine (born 1935)
charcoal and pencil on paper
and photomontage
TIME, January 4, 1982

John Updike born 1932
by Alex Katz (born 1927)
oil on canvas
TIME, October 18, 1982

Ronald Reagan born 1911
and Yuri Andropov 1914–1984
Men of the Year
by Alfred Leslie (born 1927)
oil on canvas
TIME, January 2, 1984

Michael Jackson born 1958
by Andy Warhol (1928–1987)
oil and silkscreen on canvas
TIME, March 19, 1984

Vladimir Horowitz 1904–1990
by R. B. Kitaj (born 1932)
pastel on paper
TIME, May 5, 1986

John Gotti born 1940
by Andy Warhol (1928–1987)
silkscreen on colored paper
TIME, September 29, 1986

David Byrne born 1952
self-portrait
photo collage
TIME, October 27, 1986

Deng Xiaoping 1904–1997
Man of the Year
by Robert Rauschenberg (born 1925)
photo collage
TIME, January 6, 1986

Mikhail Gorbachev born 1931
Man of the Year
by Nikolai Soloninkin (born 1945)
papier-mâché box
TIME, January 4, 1988
TIME *magazine, New York City*

Wrapped Globe, 1988
Planet of the Year
by Christo (born 1935)
photograph by Gianfranco Gorgoni
plastic, polyethylene rope, and globe
TIME, January 2, 1989
TIME *magazine, New York City*

"I Love New York"
by Roger Brown (1941–1997)
oil on canvas
TIME, September 17, 1990
TIME *magazine, New York City*

"Women: The Road Ahead"
by Susan Moore (born 1953)
oil pastel, paint stick, and acrylic
on paper
TIME, special issue, fall 1990
TIME *magazine, New York City*

Jay Leno born 1950
by Al Hirschfeld (born 1903)
pen and ink on paper
TIME, March 16, 1992
TIME *magazine, New York City*

Bill Clinton born 1946
by C. F. Payne (born 1954)
watercolor, ink, acrylic, and
oil on board
TIME, February 22, 1993

Pope John Paul II born 1920
Man of the Year
by Richard Selesnick and
Nicholas Kahn (both born 1964)
fresco
TIME, January 2, 1995
TIME *magazine, New York City*